JUST TA.

I do not know why humans truly do not put God first. Many say they love God yet, refuse to listen to sound advice – that which God is trying to show them life wise, spiritually, future wise, and more.

God is not a religion or politician. God is the Creator of Life that do all to protect the Children and People of Life. Right now, humans are truly not living for life because evil control us, rule us; govern us business wise, politically, religiously, and no matter how God show us this, we as humans cannot see it. We believe instead of knowing.

Right now, humans are poor mentally, spiritually, and life wise.

BRIGHTER DAY *by the Reggae Artist Bushman*

As humans, we fail to realize that:
IF WE DO NOT KNOW GOD, GOD CANNOT KNOW US.

IF WE DO NOT PUT OUR TRUST IN GOD, HOW CAN GOD TRUST US?

IF YOU CANNOT LIVE WITH SELF; HOW CAN YOU LIVE WITH GOD, AND OTHERS?

IF ALL WE ARE GIVEN IS/ARE LIES; WE/YOU CAN ONLY LIVE BY LIES. WE/YOU

CANNOT KNOW THE TRUTH, OR LIVE IN OR BY THE TRUTH.

God has been trying but it is us as humans that are truly not listening. We put others over God.

As humans we break all the Law and Laws of Life?

As humans we do as we want without thinking of life; our life with self, others, and God.

There is a life beyond the physical, and this life is determined by each human here on Earth and not God. God do not interfere in the life of the wicked and evil this I know for a fact without doubt but, billions of you truly do not know this.

We burn our roads, and bridges with God then expect God to save us in the end; why?

Religious lies cannot save you.
Political lies cannot save you.
Judicial lies cannot save you.
Historical lies cannot save you.
Musical lies cannot save you.
Belief cannot and will never save you.
Family lies cannot save you.
Generational lies cannot save you.
The lies you tell cannot save you.

You of you is the one to save you. Listen, IF YOU CANNOT COME CLEAN WITH SELF; HOW CAN YOU COME CLEAN WITH GOD, AND OTHERS?

If "TRUTH IS EVERLASTING LIFE;" how come we are living in lies here on Earth with self, family, God, and others?

2

If _"TRUTH IS EVERLASTING LIFE;"_ how come we are not living by the truth?

Can anyone function without life?
Can anyone live without life?

Some are saying; yes to you can function without life, and live without life. But; what is life to you?

Are you living?

Are you not dying – going to die physically and spiritually if your name is written in the Book of Death?

How many of you globally have and has made Truth; the True and Living God your Life and World?

Now hear me now. Many of us say we are good, but how good are we?

AS EVIL IS TO BLAME FOR ALL THAT IS HAPPENING HERE ON EARTH. _THE GOOD AND TRUE OF LIFE ARE TO BE BLAMED AS WELL._

No, it's wha?

It's not; how dare you blame the Good and True of Life?

Don't say it; that I am sick in the head, and I am not of God. You cannot blame the Good and True of Life for all that is happening here on Earth.

And I am telling you, _I CAN, AND DID._

Shhh!!!!

Are you in an environment that is segregated from all who are wicked and evil?

Are you working in an environment that honour and respect Life – the Truth of Life – God including, you, ad others?

Are you living the life God want and need you to live?

Don't with the churches you are in because, you know you are in the Domain of Death if you are in the Churches of Death.

How often as a good person do you store up your truth and life in God?

Are you not living wrong because you are not in a clean environment?

How many people have you told about these books in hope of helping You, Me, and God to secure the right and true environment God need you to be in with God?

What Good God Values have you instilled in your Children and Grandchildren?

How often do you go out with God?

How often do you shop in stores set up by clean, true, and good people?

How often do you buy from clean, good, and true Black People?

How often do you secure the clean finances of the good and true so that truth rise good and true?

How often do you secure your good, clean, and true finances, health, home, God, and more?

Do you even send your children to the Schools of the good and true?

How often do you fight against the good and true, and cause them to fail because you are loyal to Death; Evil?

Nope, you are......

A good and true person do not think of their monetary gain alone. They think of you and help those who help them to live right, rise, and attain God.

Aye, Marcus Mosiah Garvey and his efforts, and what we as Black People did for him not to secure a home for many of you in Africa.

Aye, Robert Nesta Marley, aka Bob Marley. Despite his wrongs, he did try to educate you yet, you as Blacks refused the message he gave to the lots of you in; Redemption Song, Babylon System, Time Will Tell, Natural Mystic, Could You Be Loved, and more.

And truly don't say you can't go out with God because you can. All you have to do is say; "God, I am going on the road for a walk, to get groceries, to wash my dirty clothes, walk with me, or drive with me?"

So, yes, as Black People we need to change from our <u>CONDITIONED THINKING OF GOD, WHO GOD IS, WHO WE ARE, AND MORE.</u>

We have to change from our conditioned thinking as to what constitutes Life and Death including, Truth.

Belief is of Man and not God.

Knowledge is of God thus, Man – Humans cannot comprehend God or the thinking, and talk of God.

If you don't speak – talk to God; how can God speak, or talk to you?

If you do not acknowledge God, how can God acknowledge you?

You of yourself know that; EVIL DO NOT LIKE GOD.

You of yourself know that; EVIL MUST DESTROY ALL THE GOODNESS OF GOD. So, now tell me; what have you done to preserve the Life of God here on Earth?

What have you done to preserve you with God?

And no, going to church Monday, Wednesday, Sunday, or Monday, Friday, Saturday, or which ever day you go to Church cannot preserve your life, or save you from Death.

ABSOLUTELY NO ONE CAN FIND GOD; THE TRUE AND LIVING GOD IN ANY CHURCH.

If Death is your God then yes, you will find your God; Death in your church or wherever you pray.

Take the time to know you. Thus, take the time for silence. Without true silence you cannot hear the surroundings around you.

Listen, we can live without traffic. Traffic – the cars – automotive vehicles running day and night is a hindrance to life because none

6

adhere to silence. Therefore, the automotive industry contributes to you not hearing God and your surroundings.

Take the time to live with you and by yourself, and you will begin to know, and find God; all the truth you need.

You are out of your toxic relationship. Live with you for a while. I know sex will be hard for some of you especially if your life is based on Sex, and Sexual Gratification, but give your body a break to heal; clean you from her odour; his odour; their odour if you were in more than one relationship.

Clean the aura around you.

If you cannot live with you, you most definitely cannot live with God. This I know for a fact without doubt. Therefore, I am telling you, learn to live with yourself and by yourself.

God is Silence, *and God is alone.* You will not get God is alone, but you will over time.

Take the time to let go of all the negatives in your life.

There is Physical and Spiritual Wickedness and if you do not know what constitutes, Physical and Spiritual Wickedness then you are lost.

More is to come here on Earth and if you are not prepared for the WHAT'S TO COME; how are you going to survive?

If we as humans continue to let Evil govern – rule and control us today, how are you going to live tomorrow when all comes full force here on Earth?

As Good People, you can no longer live by the Ways of your Evil Politicians, Religious Leaders, Gang Leaders, Corporate Demons that control the Global Marketplace, and more.

When we as the Good and True of Life buy from the Wicked and Evil of Life, we are giving away our prosperity with God.

When we as the Good and True of Life do not set up Good Foundations and Frameworks with God, we are denying God us, and our Truth.

When we as the Good and True of Life do not set up Good and True Businesses here on Earth, we are denying God our Good Prosperity – the goodness God is waiting to shower us with.

When we live in Lands of Evil, we are denying us and God Life all around.

<u>Know:</u>

<u>IT IS FORBIDDEN FOR GOOD TO BE INTEGRATED WITH EVIL.</u>

<u>When Good integrates with Evil, Evil takes us from Life – make us dirty as them.</u>

Therefore, it is wise to surround yourself with good, true, and clean people.

It is wise to buy from good, true, and clean people.

Right now, Evil is prospering off you the Good and True.

When we the Good and True buy from Evil Companies, Corporations, Stores; we are not only giving away our prosperity; we are being weakened as well as, giving away our life. Therefore, seek goodness and truth all the time if you are good and true.

Yes, I know it's hard to find clean people to buy from thus, ask God to help you. If you have a store and you are good, run your store, and life good and true.

If goodness cannot rise, how can we as the Good and True say we are going to live with God?

Goodness truly builds and so does God. So, why are you as the Good and True not helping God and yes, me to build us good and true for a Brighter, and Better Tomorrow?

Know that; God did not tell anyone Good to integrate with or, live with the wicked and evil of Earth. *In all God has done, God has been trying to keep the Children and People of Life out of the Devil's domain here on Earth and in the Spiritual Realm. It is us as the Good and True – Children and People of Life that refuse to listen to God.*

Evil is not in the Domain of Life with God, therefore, as the Good and True, Evil must not, and should not be in the Life and World of the Good and True here on Earth.

Evil will always seek to destroy God, therefore, evil lie on the True and Living God thus, humans truly do not see, or comprehend the lies of Man's so-called holy bible.

Listen, I see things via my dreams, waking state visions, and more. You are my outlet of truth. Meaning, <u>do good for you and by you by helping me to spread the Message of God despite the way you feel.</u>

God is my Source of Power and Truth.

God is a part of my Good and True Life.

All that is happening here on Earth and going to happen here on Earth is due to humans and not God. As humans; You do not <u>ELECT TRUTH TO GOVERN AND OVERSEE YOU.</u>

Yes, I take myself out of this because I go to God with all thus, I do not vote, or go to church – the Domains of Death. I went to God truthfully and asked for forgiveness for all my wrongs and more done unto God.

I know the truth and I have to keep the truth.

I cannot be anyone else but me thus, I have my True Bank Account, Chequing/Checking Account, Savings Account, and More with God. And yes, I need a True Savings Account with Mother Earth because she Mother Earth is a true part of life despite her housing Death; the Death of Flesh in her.

Listen, if you do not have goodness and truth to govern and oversee you, you cannot have life, you can only have death and billions here on Earth have and has Death. Thus, billions are written out of the Book of Life. Meaning, your name is not in the Book of Life, but in the Book of Death.

Michelle
February 2021

I do not know why people would leave things at the last minute to fix self Lovey. With my dream of seeing your Green Train and White People trying to get on your train, why would they; White People want or need access to your World and Kingdom after they've done so much wrong in life not just in the Physical Realm but in the Spiritual Realm as well?

If the White Race wanted and needed Life, would they not have lived for Life?

Why would they deceive nations with their lies and deceit?

You've destroyed life here on Earth including the Life of Earth then want to be saved; why?

You cannot do all to destroy then want life. This makes absolutely no sense Life Wise.

Why destroy Life then want Life when you've done all to destroy Life?

Go to Hell and die because Life was not your truth and goal; Death was.

How can you as a Race and People lie on the True and Living God then have the gaul to want God – the True and Living God to save you?

Why do all to kill then?
Why not think of your life?
Why not think of the life of others?
Why not think of the Life of God?

Why not think of the Life of Earth?

No Lovey. What do you mean to these people?
What is your life's worth to these people?

Why give up life if you did not want to die?

Life isn't about greed; all you can achieve here on Earth with your lies, deceit, greed, and more.

You as a Race and People stood against Life – All Life. Stay standing against Life and not want to be saved because truth was never ever your stay come on now.

No Lovey, I cannot have mercy for the merciless.

No Lovey, like I tell you, I will not plea to you for Black Sell Outs. Why the hell should I plea to you for White Sell Outs?

No, I will not let my anger take fold. We Lovey are talking consciously here.

You treat the different races like shit; crap of shit especially the Black Race now you want compassion for the evils you've done unto other races including the Black Race. How does that work?

You've hurt so many including Earth and God. Were you thinking of the consequences of your actions when you were doing all that is evil unto others?

So, why should Any Saved in Life look to your race and save the lots of you?

Why should God save any of you?

What goodness did any of you over the ages add to Life, and the Life of God?

No, you are an entitled Race of People.

With all the wrongs you've done, you cannot accept the wrongs you've done here on Earth.

Answer me this. Were your actions not spiteful and without regard for the other races especially the Black Race?

How many have you manipulated and killed in the Black Race with your lies, deceit, religious lies, political lies, judicial lies, diseases you created and manufactured here on Earth to take the life of others, and more?

Now that things is/are reaching Critical Mass, you are going to seek refuge in God.

God should have been your refuge from the get go.

God did not put enmity in your life against anyone thus, you lie on the True and Living God then expect the God of Life you turned against to save you.

Wow to your entitlement.

You turned nations – billions against Life – God so, why should God look at your Race and save the lots of you?

Look at Earth and the ill things your race has and have done to Earth. So, why should Earth have compassion for any of you, or even save you by pleading to God for the lots of you?

Why should Earth herself have compassion for any of you, or even save you with all the ill things you've done in her?

You kept Death in her.

You spilled blood on land with your murderous ways and still, you can't learn that God will never be with anyone unclean.

Billions you've caused to forfeit life with your lies and religious lies and still, you want a saved and or, God to save you, and the lots of you.

You made sacrifices unto Death and still you want Life to save you!!!!!

You sacrificed Earth to Death.
You caused Earth to not be able to expand due to your lies; ills.

You made nations follow your lies thus, taking Good and True Life from Earth come on now.

Did any of you think of the pain you caused God?
Did any of you think of the pain you caused Earth?

Did any of you think of the pain you were causing others here on Earth?

Life is truly not about control, nor is life about sending anyone to Hell to die come on now.

Michelle
February 2021

Lovey, Mother Earth, All, never mind because I truly do not know why Black People feel as if the White Way of Life is the right and or, best way of life.

I still cannot comprehend why anyone would give up their life to die alongside their enemies.

No Lovey, I cannot see what life can anyone have in Hell?

I am at a loss right now Lovey thus, I cannot comprehend the logic of Man; Men.

Can a man produce life on their own Lovey?

I so don't know today, and I am so going to leave things alone. My mind is on a different level with You and Mother Earth. There is so much that I want and need to do with the both of you here on Earth yet, cannot do that which I need to do with the both of you.

PUT LOVE FIRST by Sweet C.

I so don't know what to write so I am going to leave things alone. My mind is truly elsewhere.

Right now, I need a world and place for me that is independent of the environment I am in. Thus, at times my world is like a fairy tale with Lovey; God.

I have to truly put my trust and true love in Lovey. I need truth right now. Therefore, I am going to send Lovey to the song above by Sweet C, and all the questions Sweet C pose in this song, I am going to pose them to Lovey.

No everyone, I want to know if Lovey would let me go or find me, and bring me back into his and or, her arms and world.

16

Lovey knows I will not leave, but I need to know the extent of God's Jealousy when it comes to me. So yes, I am putting God on the spot right now.

Certain things I know Lovey would not allow me to do this I know for a fact without doubt, but I need to know the extent of God's Jealousy and True Love when it comes to me.

No everyone, I am this way with Lovey.

Listen, I am expecting Lovey to truly defend me so that when my enemies come upon to harm me Lovey sey, oh, a suh. Bladaff, Bax Dung, Kick Dung. Michelle is mine therefore, trouble her not because she is not troubling you.

Trust me, it would more than make my day and world if Lovey could truly defend me this way here on Earth, and in the Spiritual Realm. Thus, I will forever tell you, I live in a Fairy Tale World with Lovey.

So yes, when I am having a horrible day, I am expecting Lovey to comfort me, and put me above all my troubles. Yes, I need right life – the perfect and right world with God here on Earth with Mother Earth. There is a better place out there, but this perfect and right world I truly do not know how to create and gain here on Earth.

There is so much that I truly do not know.

How do I create my own world void of wicked and evil humans – all that is undesirable to me?

Yes, for now all I can do is write and think of a better and perfect world with God.

It's hard for me because there is no portal that I can escape through where I leave this world of pain, sorrow, greed, human destruction, religious lies, political lies, corporate lies, family lies, historical lies, generational lies, lies told on God, and more behind.

Right now, I need my all to be good and true as well as, stress free.

Yes, I need Lovey to rescue me from my thoughts and show me what I need to do to fulfill my life and world with him and or, her.

Right knowledge is true, and I truly need this. There is something out there that I need to find when it comes to creation; reaching God without limits.

I truly hate being limited God Wise. Meaning, not knowing how to connect with God where I can just walk away from life here on Earth as I am without the shedding of Flesh and Spirit.

Yes, I have my dreams but having dreams is truly not enough for me. I need to connect with God and truly sit and talk to God.

There is so much that I want and need to do, and I truly need God with me to do all that I need to do here on Earth.

Michelle
February 2021

ROMAN CATHOLIC CHURCH DREAM

Dear God please take hold of me because what I just saw dream wise is truly not great.

Lovey, it's February 9, 2021 and what am I seeing?

It's like today and the past in one.

God have mercy. Truly have mercy upon me.
Have mercy because, I truly do not know what's going on.

Dreamt people were protesting but I did not see the people who were protesting. Apparently, they won their protest and all I saw was a numberless amount of people; like army people bowing down to the ground with spears.

Seeing the numberless amount of people bowing down to the ground with their spears, I wondered to myself in the dream if I was wrong about protest; people protesting.

Seeing that; the numberless amount of people bowing down to the ground with spears and thinking if I was wrong about protest, I was someplace else. It's like I was back in time because I was amongst people, numberless amount of people. I was walking through these people; numberless amount of people and or, numberless crowd. This crowd were a crowd – numberless amount of Church People; Roman Catholic People. They were celebrating. I do not know if it's their Pope or Priest, but I would say either or. They were celebrating his birthday apparently.

Weaving through the crowd, the Pope and or, Priest was high up on a Mount because this place was high up. The Pope and or, Priest was preaching. To the right of him was this building I would say old Rome and or, Greek building. I wanted to go into the building, but when I saw the cross atop the building, I refrained from going into the building. The cross I would not say

19

was wooden, but tall and brown but not brass. I checked Google for the type of cross I saw but none I saw was like the cross I saw in my dream.

So, this Pope and or, Priest was speaking; preaching and or, talking about Jesus, and I said to myself in the dream; "does he not know that Jesus was Black?"

And yes, it was an older Priest and or, Pope preaching to a numberless crowd of people.

Not listening to his speech, I went up further because I wanted to look over the precipice of the mount this Priest ad or, Pope was behind.

When I saw behind him, it was a Valley – "THE VALLEY OF DEATH," I would call it. All I saw was the Bodies of Children encased in shrines – white casket shrines. The children were laying on their back. The face and body of the children was encased in these shrines. Further, the Bodies of the Children where laying in a line going head to feet/foot.

Seeing that, I saw one as if his body was a statue – the head and shoulder of a statue. I kept going and this girl – white girl was singing this song – beautiful song, and I got a book and pen and began to write down some of the lyrics of the song she was singing. Please note; in the dream, you heard the song but did not see the white girl that was singing the song.

I will not analyze this dream because I know, and I truly do not know what to make of it.

But dear God, do humans not know the Precipice of Death of the Roman Catholic Church?

Lovey and God, Allelujah, the church has and has led the People; numberless amounts of people to their deaths, and still people run behind their priests and popes thinking they can be saved; are going to be saved.

Lovey, the Precipice of Death and or, Valley of Death.

Why did you show me this Precipice of Death?
Lovey the Precipice look nice – green but really Lovey?

This valley is deep.

I've seen precipice before Lovey, but I've never seen this Precipice before; this Precipice is of Old. Dear God, how wicked is the Roman Catholic Church that people cannot see that Rome, and the Roman Catholic Church is of Death? Lovey, Rome and the Roman Catholic work for Death; are of Death.

I see the death of children Lovey; White Children.

Now I ask you Lovey. How many kids from the past until now have the Roman Catholic Church – their Priests, and Popes have and has literally killed?

How many Black Children have they used and abused; killed from then until now Lovey?

Lovey, I saw the line of Death.

Dear God, how do you cope in seeing this?

21

Absolutely no one can progress in live when it comes to the Roman Catholic Church and Religion; any church or religion.

Lovey, how can people think they are worshiping you when Priests and Popes commit atrocious acts of Death – killing?

Have humans pegged you that disgusting Lovey?

Have humans pegged you that disgusting to allow demons to oversee them?

No, don't answer that Lovey. Humans peg you that disgusting because billions think they are worshipping you, but are worshipping Death.

<u>Now let me ask you this Lovey. Why Jesus?</u>

<u>Why do the White Race and the different races use the Name of Jesus?</u>

Many think Jesus; thus, it's the Church that Preach of Jesus – Death.

Jesus is Death yet, billions cannot figure this out yet.

*So yes, <u>**billions are going to die literally because Death is their God.**</u>*

Billions do not know that they are bowing down to Death Lovey.

Billions do not know the God the Church, and the different Races come to believe in is Death.

Billions truly do not know that the God they are given by the different Churches of the Globe is Death.

22

Billions truly do not know that they are Hell Bound literally.

And no Lovey, I truly don't want to speak about Jesus because, the Jesus people believe in, and think is of you Lovey is truly Death. JESUS DIED. *Therefore, many do not know the truth.*

Billions are going to die like their God Jesus. Thus, billions live to die instead of living to live.

Many do not know that:

ABSOLUTELY NO ONE CAN DIE AND SEE LIFE - YOU LOVEY. THEY HAVE TO; MUST LIVE TO SEE LIFE; YOU LOVEY.

In order for anyone to see you Lovey; THEIR NAME MUST BE IN THE BOOK OF LIFE. THAT PERSON MUST BE OF LIFE.

NO DEATH CAN SEE LIFE BECAUSE, LIFE AND DEATH IS DIFFERENT IN SO MANY WAYS.

LIFE AND DEATH IS SEPARATE IN THE TRUEST OF SENSE.

NO ONE THAT IS OF LIFE CAN SEE DEATH ONCE THE SPIRIT SHED THE FLESH.

THEREFORE, <u>JESUS WAS NOT OF LIFE BECAUSE HE DIED.</u> GAVE UP HIS LIFE TO DEATH TO SAVE THE WICKED AND EVIL.

<u>BUT IN GIVING UP HIS LIFE TO SAVE THE WICKED AND EVIL; JESUS SAVED NONE,</u> AND THIS BILLIONS TRULY DO NOT KNOW.

IF JESUS WAS OF LIFE, <u>HE WOULD HAVE KNOWN THAT NO CHILD OF LIFE CAN GIVE UP THEIR LIFE TO DEATH.</u>

<u>NO CHILD OF GOD – ANY CHILD THAT IS OF GOD CAN DIE OR, GIVE UP THEIR LIFE TO SAVE DEATH'S CHILDREN AND PEOPLE.</u>

<u>It is forbidden for Life – any child and or, the children and People of Life to take from Death.</u>

<u>LIFE CANNOT DIE ONLY DEATH – THOSE WHO BELONG TO DEATH CAN</u>

DIE – WILL DIE. DEATH OWN THEM, AND THEIR NAME IS IN THE BOOK OF DEATH.

Thus, it's on the shedding of flesh that many know their Life and or, Death.

So yes Lovey, **the BELIEFS OF MAN – MEN – HUMANS DO CAUSE THEM TO DIE LITERALLY.**

The truth must be known Lovey, but why this Army – why were these people conceding – bowing down.

Why concede to Death?

Why give up your life to Death in this way?

Questions I have Lovey because I truly do not know about this dream. **Why are the Churches of the Globe painting this pretty picture of Heaven when we; You and I Lovey know that Heaven for the Churches of the Globe is Hell?**

Everything for the Church is Good, of Faith, and Belief yet, **HUMANS CANNOT SEE THE PRECIPICE OF HELL BEHIND THE DIFFERENT CHURCHES OF THE GLOBE.**

I so do not want or need this book to be too long Lovey because, I am at a loss as to what I see. My countenance is truly down because of what I see.

25

Lovey, when will the Churches of the Globe fail – fall?

When will people globally wake up and realize that they've been scammed big time by the different Churches of the Globe?

When will people – humans globally wake up and realize that; *NO CHURCH, NO PRIEST, NO PASTOR, NO POPE, NO DEACON, NO PREACHER, AND MORE THAT SAY THEY ARE HOLY REPRESENT LIFE; YOU LOVEY?*

They all represent Death. Therefore, every member of their congregation was, and is their sacrifice unto Death literally.

Billions are Hell Bound Lovey. Now tell me. Is this what humans globally truly wanted for self?

Wow.

Lovey, was this what you perceived for humans in that way when it comes to the Different Churches of the Globe?

I know, that was a stupid question on my part Lovey, but I have to ask.

How and why did the Church become so powerful that they use You Lovey to manipulate, and lie to Nations?

Why let the Different Churches of the Globe use You Lovey as their scapegoat to mislead, and deceive people?

Lovey, Death has gained billions of lives.

Life cannot take from Death yet, Death can take from Life Lovey; why? No, that is wrong Michelle. Death cannot take from Life. Death take that which is of Death. Life is truly not of Death therefore, Death cannot take from Life in this way or in any way.

Wow Lovey because, the more I live is the more I learn, and see literally.

Lovey, why are people so easily manipulated when it comes to Religion, Politicians, and others?

Why is power and control the mainstay for some?
What good is in power and control apart from slavery?

Is it right for people to live in controlled environments Lovey?
Is it right for others – people to control people?

You Lovey do not choose Life or Death for anyone so, why do humans let other choose Death for them?

Michelle

I so do not know what to write today. It's like my brain is on go slow.

Have questions but do not know how to go about it. My mindset is truly different. I am trying to formulate Black People if that is even possible to formulate Black People.

Wrong wording yes, but not for me.

In my dream about the Roman Catholic Church above being the Domain of Death – The Dead. How do Black People here on Earth comprehend this?

Why do we as Black People continually go into the Domains of Death thinking we can find Life?

Why do we as Black People destroy our self for naught – a place in hell?

We know the White Race's Way is not our way and true way yet as Blacks, we continually sacrifice our self and future for a place in hell.

Do we even look into self and all around us and say, why are we living this way; false, because of other races?

Do we truly look into self and all around us and say, why are we dying the White Way?

Do we truly look into self and all around us and say, why do we as Black People have to give up our Black God to attain Death?

Do we even say; why do we have to accept Death in order to have Life?

Is Death not Death, and Life not Life?

Once you are Dead, you cannot have Life. So, in all the White Race write and tell; all is a lie.

<u>*If God – the God – Jesus they; the White Race gave humans – all of humanity died, then; "DEATH WOULD HAVE BEEN GREATER THAN LIFE, AND GOD – THE GOD THEY; THE WHITE RACE GAVE US IS WEAK; THE BITCH OF DEATH BECAUSE, DEATH TOOK THE LIFE OF GOD THUS, MAKING DEATH SUPERIOR TO LIFE."*</u>

So, who is God to man – humans if; we believe all that is nasty when it comes to God?

As humans, we truly do not know God. If we did, then all the crap of shit – dung religion feed us and say is of God, we would condemn.

We as humans would see that religion is truly not clean, and can never be clean.

We as humans would see that no religion represents Life – all that is clean, and of God.

Now I ask you. If we as humans believe all that is nasty when it comes to God. How should God feel?

Why should God save any of us?

As you can see, I can go back in the past via my dream world. I see the past, present, and future. Now I ask you.

IF WE AS BLACK PEOPLE KNOW THAT THE ROMAN CATHOLIC CHURCH DEFY LIFE; IS THE DOMAIN – VALLEY OF DEATH; WHY ARE YOU AS BLACK PEOPLE GOING INTO THE DOMAIN OF DEATH?

WHY ARE YOU AS BLACK PEOPLE SENDING YOUR CHILDREN TO ROMAN CATHOLIC SCHOOLS?

WHY ARE YOU AS BLACK PEOPLE ALLOWING AND LETTING THE DEMONS OF THE ROMAN CATHOLIC CHURCH BAPTIZE, AND CHRISTEN YOUR CHILDREN – BABIES?

WHY SACRIFICE YOUR CHILDREN TO DEATH IN THIS WAY?

You see and know the atrocities of the Roman Catholic Church and Rome from the Past to the Present including Tomorrow, and all in the Black Community is telling God that they prefer the Nasty Way – Death's Way of Life.

Why are we as humans disrespecting God – the True God of Life in this way?

Many of you see and know the nastiness of the Churches yet, still stay in this nastiness hoping God is going to save you.

COME OUT OF THE NASTINESS OF DEATH – THE CHURCHES, AND REPENT OF YOUR SIN WITH GOD IN THIS WAY.

LET GOD; THE GOD OF LIFE WIPE YOU SLATE CLEAN OF DEATH WITH HIM OR HER.

ABSOLUTELY NO ONE CLEAN CAN GO IN THE DOMAIN OF DEATH EXPECTING TO FIND GOD BECAUSE; GOD TRULY DO NOT ALLOW THE CHILDREN AND PEOPLE OF LIFE ACCESS TO THE DOMAINS – CHURCHES OF DEATH.

In all I know; God do keep the Children and People of Death out of the Domain of Death – the Churches in this way.

We cannot say; *"GOD I WANT AND NEED LIFE," AND GO INTO THE CHURCHES OF DEATH, AND DISPRECT YOURSELF, AND GOD."*

You cannot Love God, you have to truly Love God. God do not deal in Love. God deals in Truth. Therefore, God only deal in True Love.

It's 2021 therefore, the Love So of Old with Lovey and God truly do not work.

As humans we have to truly respect our self and God. We cannot call on God then go to Death and give your Blessings – the Blessings God has and have given you to Death.

You know you cannot find Life in Death, so why are we as Black People in Churches?

I truly can't think on this day the way I need to think. The music I am listening to is truly not helping me right now. Many in the Black Community know the truth yet, distort the truth in their Music for real.

Blacks are falling and none can see that the System and Systems of Lies they believe in is truly killing them.

Blacks still have not realized that; "<u>**AS BLACKS YOU CANNOT BELIEVE IN GOD. YOU HAVE TO KNOW GOD.**</u>"

Belief is truly not knowledge. So, if you do not know God, you cannot be saved.

GOD IS NOT BELIEF.

GOD IS KNOWLEDGE.

ALL KNOWING.

CREATION.

CREATOR.

TEACHER.

PROTECTOR.

DIVINE.

HOLY.

TRUE.

CLEAN.

TRUE LOVE.

OUR TRUE LIFE SOURCE, AND MORE.

Wow.

My head is truly not there. Now I want to change the tempo in this book without notice.

So, would you have breakfast with me?
Walk with me?
Hold my hand?
Clothe me?
Feed me?
Be the all I need for that moment?

Call me, no, you can't call me. You do not have my phone number, nor do I have a cell phone, or cell number to give you.

You can email me. I do have a email account. But I don't want to give it to you in this book.

Find me, because some of my other books do have my email address in it.

Seek and ye shall find in this way.

When you do find. No nasty emails because if I clap back trust me, you will not like how far I will go. Cussing is engrained in me therefore, when Jamaicans cuss you, you are well cussed out. We hold nothing back. So, be warned. I do cuss, and I will take it that far if you truly piss me off in that way.

Your ancestral history will come into play too.

It's February, and I don't want to write Poetry and dedicate them to God or my gorgeous and beautiful Mother including, Mother Earth.

Mother Earth and Lovey truly know what I want and need to do, but we will see. I will let you know if I did what I wanted to do with God and Mother Earth.

So, breakfast for two?
You and me?
Lunch and dinner too?

Yes, yes, yes, coffee for two.

You can have tea but not for two.
Not you and me.

Smile, my tea is truly different.

Do I make you breakfast?
Do we go out?
Have take out?
Take in for some.

Wait, wait, wait.

No, it's just me and you.
Yes, the mood is different.
Tone; atmosphere set.

Oh dear, I did not ask.

Do you like a fluffy – big girl?

Oh dear, you're thinking.

Yes, the question you are asking is; well, how big?

And I'm telling you big.

Now let me change the tone; mood again.

In life we come in different packages.

Some are small
Some medium
Some large
Some extra large
Some extra, extra large
Some huge

Well, I'm huge, and I truly love me.

Truly love all about me.
I have to be me.
Have to live with me.
Have to live for me.
Please me.

Not all are the same. Thus, I am different, and so are you.

My mood has not changed.

Well, it's changed a bit because I have a smile on my face listening to D'Franco's song <u>Forever Yours.</u>

I am going to keep it Tanya Stephens now.

For some it's <u>BIG NINJA BIKE</u> by Tanya Stephens

For some it's <u>BOOM WUK</u> by Tanya Stephens.

I had to put Boom Wuk in there. And no, I do not promote promiscuity of any kind, but like I said, it's the Boom Wuk for some. Listen, if I had the oil in my back like sum a demya young girls wow. Thus, I truly love the Mr. Killa OIL IT CHOREOGRAPHY by Wendell Bullen and Royal G.

Hey, mi a cow foot – that old, and I truly love to see the versatility of Dance in Black People literally and truly.

YU NUH READY FI DIS YET yes, by Tanya Stephens *but my ready is truly not your ready.*

Thus, many are under the SYCAMORE TREE – Lady Saw.

Some are truly freaky under the quiet. And I am so going to stop right here. Thus, Beres Hammond told you WHAT ONE DANCE CAN DO in his song, WHAT ONE DANCE CAN DO. And Janis Joplin told you in, PIECE OF MY HEART.

No, no, I have to go on.

WOMAN TO WOMAN by Shirley Brown

Hey, it could be Woman to Man.
Man to Woman.
Man to Man.
You decide.

I'LL TAKE YOU THERE – the Staple Singers.

Come on let me take you there.
Sock it to me now.

Had to put the sock it to me now in because, I wanted to be that corny going back – well, Old School.

Trust me, it's not hard to take you there.

Do you want me to set the mood again?

I do practice what I preach – teach.

So, I am going to let Barry White speak for me in this case.

<u>PRACTICE WHAT YOU PREACH</u> by Barry White.

In this case it's you that's on my mind.
The mood is set, so let me do.
I don't need to practice.
We're here.
It's me and you.
Let's do.
Come on.

Oh Lord let me stop because Valentine's Day is on Sunday February 14, 2021, and I just had my fun.

I do not have the deep voice like Barry White or a deep voice period, but if you want. No, let me keep it clean because I can write hence, I have my short stories that I so need to publish.

I so can't be serious in that way all the time. I have to take you there with me.

So, despite me being big, wow. The mind do and does take me there.

Therefore, different people have different needs and wants.

Some like the Plastic Doll Look.

Some like the Plastic Surgery Look of so-called Perfection.

Some like the Hood Look.
The Petite Look.
Medium Look.
Fluffy Look.

Your preference depends on you.
You have a type and so do I.

In this world of hate and dismay. People find something to hate on. As humans we cannot see people for who they are. No, that's not true, some of us do see people for who they are thus, Good and Evil are integrated here on Earth.

Not everyone is everyone's flavour. Therefore, I have to live by my truth and for the truth of me, God, the Saved, Mother Earth, and more.

So, with all that said; dinner for two?
Breakfast for two, or coffee for two; just you and me?

Hey, I have to be the true me in life which is different.

Michelle
February 10, 2021

It is after 6am February 13, 2021, and I can't go back to sleep.

All I have to say is Dear God have mercy on me and my soul including spirit to the dream I had.

Black American Gospel Singers, you truly do not know what you have done to self literally.

FRED HAMMOND, ANGIE STONE + DREAM

Dreamt Fred Hammond, Angie Stone, <u>this Black Actor</u> that I do not know his name, but he does television movies for the Lifetime Network I believe. I tried finding his picture on Google but could not find it. I am also going to include Radical For Christ here because they sing with Fred Hammond.

In the dream, I was somewhere but I cannot tell you exactly where. I truly do not know. All I know is, I was seeing American Gospel Singers, and this American I would say Christian Actor.

In the dream, there was a concert and Fred Hammond who would not listen in the dream took to the stage and began to sing to this massive crowd of people. It's as if the place lit up with light while Fred Hammond sang on stage to the massive crowd of people that could not be numbered. This light covered Fred Hammond and the people. To me they were down – the stage and people were not up but down. A mini pit then.

Seeing that, I was now outside on land and none could see the <u>MUCUS OF THE TEARS THAT WAS SHED ON LAND.</u>

<u>The Mucus was a lot so, I took a clear jug with water to try to wash the Mucus away but could not.</u> *Therefore, I truly do not know what is going*

39

to happen to Black Americans because, their hell is going to be more than they can bare literally.

Now as at February 22, 2021, and editing this book the Black Actor with Fred Hammond, and Angie Stone that I saw in the dream was/is <u>**Lamman Rucker.**</u> *Therefore, God is good all the time. When I thought all hope was gone for finding this gentleman, I found him. I saw his face on the internet for the movie* <u>*First Impression.*</u>

Oh God the Precipice, the precipice, the precipice.

Oh God I cannot go on with the dream because; <u>**BLACK CHRISTIANS IN AMERICA, AND GLOBALLY TRULY DO NOT KNOW WHAT THEY HAVE DONE.**</u>

Allelujah, have mercy because many of you are in the Precipice of Hell, and literally do not know. Hell has the lots of you and there is no escaping hell for many of you.

I cannot go on with this dream because Death is coming your way – and the Mucus of Tears is your hell because, more Black People are going to die and go to hell literally.

I truly do not want to think of some radical psychopath taking the lives of many at a Gospel Concert or any Concert for real.

Hell must come down to Earth and trust me, <u>*"MANY BLACK PEOPLE ARE GOING TO WEEP BECAUSE, THE INIQUITIES OF THE*</u>

AMMORITES IS NOT YET DONE." Just to quote your nasty bible.

Dear God, dear God what is it about Black People and Religion? What is it about Black People that we do not listen?

What curse surrounds the Black Race that we've become so negligent with our life, and you Lovey?

What is wrong with the Black Race that Blacks have to make Hell their resting place, and home?

What is wrong with the Black Race that Blacks cannot see that they are the eliminated race thus, "HELL IS FULL OF BLACK PEOPLE, AND RECRUITING MORE."

I have seen the graves of Blacks in Hell Lovey. When are Blacks going to learn that they are hell bound?

When are Blacks going to learn, see, and know that; YOU LOVEY IS NOT A RELIGION?

When are Blacks going to learn, see, and know that; THEY HAVE TO LEAVE OUT OF THE DIFFERENT DOMAINS OF DEATH – RELIGION?

Lovey, when are Blacks going to learn that all was GIVEN TO THEM TO TAKE THEM FROM LIFE?

Blacks have and has lost their way Lovey.
Blacks have lost their way.

God, why are Blacks so stupid?
Why can't we learn that lies take us from you?

Why can't we as Blacks learn that the <u>**WHITE MAN'S GOD IS NOT YOU LOVEY?**</u>

Lovey where do I start with an <u>**IGNORANT RACE OF PEOPLE THAT LIVE THE WHITE WAY OF LIFE?**</u>

Where do I start with an <u>**IGNORANT RACE OF PEOPLE THAT WILLING GIVE UP THEIR LIFE FOR DEATH?**</u>

<u>**LOVEY WHAT'S WRONG WITH YOU?**</u> *And yes, I am screaming.*

What is wrong with Life – You Lovey that we as Blacks continually FORFEIT LIFE WITH YOU?

What's so wrong with Life – You Lovey that we as Blacks have to put all that is wrong – false about self, and You Lovey?

Dear God, the Precipice of Hell when it comes to Religion yet, people cannot see that Religion lock them to/an in Hell thus, taking their Spiritual, and Physical Life from them.

<u>**RELIGION IS HELL – THE DEVIL'S WAY YET, BILLIONS CANNOT SEE THIS.**</u>

Lovey, all I need right now is a Safe Haven for me and the Saved right now.

I know you are not a religion, and can never be a religion therefore, you stay out of the Domain and Domains of Death.

I truly do not know why we as Black People cannot leave out of the Devil's Domain.

We have to leave out of Babylon come on now.

Absolutely no one can find you in dirty places Lovey.

Absolutely no one can find you in any church, mosques, synagogues, temples, shrines, and more. So, why are people going to the Whorehouses of Death, and the Domains of Death to find you Lovey?

All you can find in the Whorehouses of Death, and the Domains of Death is death.

Oh God, I truly don't know right now so I am going to go back to lay down because music cannot soothe me right now.

Thinking of Jamie Foxx but let me leave it alone.

Life is not what it seems, and you cannot get truth and true love out of stone.

Black Americans are truly different thus, they; Black Americans are a TRULY DIFFERENT RACE OF PEOPLE. To me right now Lovey. Black Americans are truly not Black. They truly do not fall under the BLACK BANNER OF LIFE literally. Therefore, I cannot worry about them; Black Americans BECAUSE, ISRAEL DID FORFEIT THEIR LIFE WITH YOU LOVEY LITERALLY.

My head is beginning to hurt. I know Lovey, I know.

The devil and their people have to ensure the Black Race fail and with successorship going to the

<u>Mongolian Race, the devil and their people are going to do all to ensure this race; the Mongolian Race fail as well.</u>

Michelle

After writing what I wrote earlier this morning because it's after 2pm now. I went back to sleep and my dream world was wow.

Listen, something is going to happen in the heavens, sky, but I cannot tell you what. I cannot say rain is going to be rained down on Earth for more than 40 days and 40 nights. All I know is, something is truly not right in the heaven; sky.

Oh, for you that have helicopters, and airplanes that have not been in use for a while including those in use, please truly service them thoroughly because helicopters are going to crash. I do not know where, but helicopters are going to crash. So, truly service your helicopters, and airplanes globally.

Did I dream about one of my doctors?

Yes, and in the dream; he told me, "he could not do this anymore."

There is more to this dream, but I know what this dream mean sight wise. In my dream world, many times he; is around me. This White Man. So yes, he's leaving me because in the dream, I told him, "he have to do what he have to for him."

Yeah me.

So yes, in my Spiritual World, and Physical World someone is going to leave me professionally.

Come on everyone, it's time for me to truly live. I cannot take Death; Physical and Spiritual Death around me all the time. I need a true and good life change.

45

For you the Farmers of the Globe, please be vigil when it comes to your crops. I do not know if there is going to be a Parasitic Invasion, but I am dreaming something that looks like a Parasite.

There is more that I want and need to tell you, but I am not allowed.

I am not going to make this book too long because I truly do not know what the rest of February have in store for me. If I can write you poetry I will but, I truly do not know if I want to. The mood is different this year for some strange reason.

Listen, the death toll is rising therefore, the Morticians of the World should be happy. They are being fed. Death is keeping them in business literally. Therefore, their Pocketbook should be increasing; rising off you the People of the Globe more and more.

I was talking to mommy yesterday, and she was telling me more and more parents are harming their children and just this morning, my sister called me. She wants us to write a book, but she needs this book to be fiction. Though the account is true, she needs the book to be written in fiction form. She was also telling me more and more partners are abusing their partner. I also told her I saw a snip it on YouTube about Toronto's Tent City, but I did not open the video. I did not want to see it.

Yes, this is disheartening for me to see and know that Toronto has and have a Tent City.

Toronto of all places have fallen victim to injustice like the rest of the world because, people truly do not live to live anymore.

People live for greed instead of living for honesty and truth.

Thus, I say, and will forever say, and excuse my words here but;
SCREW THE DIFFERENT GOVERNMENTS OF
THE WORLD – GLOBE.

And yes, you the fool, fool people of your land are to be blamed as well. If you want and need good for yourself, elect good and true people with good governance to oversee you so that they can add good and true value to your life with You and God.

Do not elect shit – the dung and piss pots of your land to oversee you. When you do this, you are taking life from your life as well as, taking life – your life from God, and the land you are living in.

Look at the way some of you are living whilst your Political Leaders are raping you and your life. Look at the way they are living high and you are living low. How much raping of you, and killing of you should your leaders do before you the people wake up and start respecting yourself?

None – no government have a place with me or in my good and true kingdom and world with Lovey.

Every government as far as I am concerned are the Dungs of the Earth. Yes, I would go as far as saying the shit holes – Demons of Death are better than any Government Official here on Earth, and that truly do not say much for any Politician when I can put a Demon above them literally.

Screw the Canadian Government literally. I don't care if they Black List me. Crap of Dung. Instead of spending so much money on War, and Accommodating

Refugees of Different Lands. Commit to your own people. Do something to help them, and not let your own people live in tents.; in the streets. As a good governor, your good and true obligation is to your people and ensuring they are safe and secure in life come on now.

How the hell do any of you in Government sleep with yourself and your partners?

Look the bleep at your children. Now tell me. How the hell can you as a government want and need homelessness for others?

Who the hell gave birth to the lots of you?

No, don't answer that. Because not even the Demons of Hell is…no, the Demons of Hell are heartless thus, many of you live worse than the Demonic Way. Thus, Death and the Demons of Hell have the lots of you truly locked in Hell – your containment unit in hell.

You cannot put other people over your own people. The need and needs of your people is/are truly not the need and needs of other people. *Put your people, and the needs of your people first come on now.*

To you the SCUM LANDLORDS OF CANADA, people should not live in the streets or tents because they cannot pay for your overpriced sit holes you call apartments. Yes, I know some people are truly nasty, but do not put your pocketbook over someone's life come on now.

Where is the sense of fairness in your land – country?

What if the tides were turned?

48

How would you feel if you lost it all and ended up in the streets like some of the people you left homeless, and in need?

No man, humans are so BC heartless that if I could prepare a New World for the Good and True of Life only I would.

No, I am sick and tired of the heartlessness of humans and their stinking scumbag political leaders, and other leaders that abuse life – all life here on Earth. Thus, for the billions that have their name in the Book of Death, I have absolutely no compassion for literally. <u>*You are to blame for letting others value you as worthless.*</u>

Your life hath worth; value it – your life. Earth cannot continue to be run by injustice, and the heartless.

What about your life and future?

Earth must change for the better thus, the changes Earth must do for self.

No Lovey; humans are too dyam heartless period.

Thus, <u>*HUMANS CAN KISS MY NATURAL BROWN ASS WITH THEIR LOVE AND CARE BULLSHIT.*</u>

<u>*So yes, Peter Tosh was correct. FOOLS DIE FOR WANT OF WISDOM.*</u>

And yes Lovey, you are truly right and correct for only saving only over 100 million people. No Lovey, I am mad, therefore, truly forgive me for my sarcasm. Life is truly worth living, it's humans that truly don't think life is truly worth living from the way we are living here on Earth, and abusing each other.

No Lovey. Until humans make you their Truth, and True Navigator then humans will never ever be different. They will forever ever live in lies only to die in lies come on now.

Thus, whatever you as people get from the evil leaders you elect to oversee you all, you all deserve because, <u>God did not have demons; it's us as humans that have – gave birth to Demonic Demons that oversee you literally.</u>

No human as far as I am concerned respect self, their land, or God thus, Earth is the Cesspool of Death.

Michelle
February 2021

It's February 14, 2021, and I can't go back to sleep.

Happy Valentine's Day everyone.

It's snowing outside and I am wide awake. Went to bed at after 2am and now I am up writing. My dream world is stable, and I am sleeping truly peacefully again. I need true peace in my life when it comes to my sleep, and sleep pattern. Even my dog is sleeping contented and peacefully in my room which is great.

Yesterday was a happy day for me. I saw my son and I held him and cried.

God is truly good. And, I do get down on God.

I need a different spirit. A happier spirit.
A spirit that can travel the universe and more.
A spirit that truly love life and hold on to life more and more.
A spirit that say; yes, all is well with me and God; All.
A spirit that more than complete me in a good and true way.

A spirit that is void of the heaviness of Death, and the evils that surround me; well, the environment I live in day in and day out.

I need God and Mother Earth to truly complete me and fulfill my life and surrounding with true truth and happiness. Never sorrow but true joy and happiness all the time.

It's Valentine's Day People and it's snowing outside.

A good and blessed morning to you all.

I do hope your day and all your days is filled with pure joy and happiness.

I pray goodness and truth for you.

I pray all that ails you and worry you, you will find a cure; a true cure for all that ails you, and true solutions to all that worries you.

I pray that God lift you up and lift your spirit in a good and true way.

True blessings always.

Michelle

Wow

LADY SAW DREAM

Marion Hall, aka Lady Saw stop mocking God.

I just dreamt you, and although I did not see you in the dream, the dream was about you.

Many of you truly do not know the crosses you bare in the Spiritual Realm; World, and trust me, you cannot see your crosses.

Let me tell you your crosses because obviously you truly do not know them.

God is not a play thing.
God is not someone to be mocked.
God is not your scapegoat.
God is not your muse.
God is not your run from then run to then run from.
God is not your Guinea Pig.

God is true Life – the Good and Truth of Life, so Lady Saw; real name Marion Hall. Stop mocking God because you truly do not know what you are doing when it comes to God – Life. You live the life of whoredom and sell whoredom and think God is with you. God is not with you, and you should know this.

God is not your plague or the locusts in your life therefore, leave God alone. You are being warned. You are the Devil's Own therefore; stop the nonsense you are doing when it comes to God because, you are truly not Chosen; a Chosen of God. You are a Chosen of Death therefore, your Cross of Death.

<u>*Continue to mock God and death will cut your ass down and rightfully so. Do not play with my God – the God of Life. You are duly and truly warned.*</u>

Like I said, you cannot see your crosses, but I can, and I did see them; your cross and or, crosses.

Your cross and or, crosses are white balls, and within those white balls lay your cross and or, crosses. I saw the cross thus, stop mocking God. No, your cross was not easy to see, but I saw it, and I know there is more than one. Therefore, **<u>THE CROSS OF DEATH.</u>**

Stop your shegry.
Stop bullshitting people.

God do not use unclean people to speak Life.
God use clean people.

God do not use unclean people to speak to the Children and People of Life.

God use clean people – someone of Life – the Life of God.

God do not send anyone of Life into unclean places and domains. God is not a demon or toy. So, stop playing with God.

<u>*You are not the word and truth of God Marion Hall, aka Lady Saw. So, stop fooling people.*</u>

God has Laws and you violate and break all the Laws of God.

Christianity – no religion is of God.

Religion is of Death yet, you Mock God – Life; why?

What has God done to you that you have to Mock God?

Thus, your name was called saying; "Lady Saw mock God."

Stop it because you truly do not know your hell and the fire pit of hell.

There is something called Spiritual Death.

THE SOUL – FLESH OF MAN – HUMANS CANNOT FACE DEATH AND WILL NEVER FACE DEATH. IT IS YOUR SPIRIT – THAT LITTLE ENERGY IN YOU THAT FACES HELL; YOUR HELL IF YOUR NAME IS IN THE BOOK OF DEATH.

And for me to see your cross and being told that you Mock God, figure out where your name is written because it's not in the Book of Life.

Billions of you use Religion as a pass without knowing Religion is of Death. The White Man's nasty game that they gave all in humanity to further take them from Life – God. And the Black Race did fall victim of this lie thus billions swear by the Lies of Religion.

God is not dirty.
God is clean.

As simple as you think; <u>DEATH PROTECT GOD.</u> Thus, it's Death that keep evil, ad people such as you out of the Realm of God.

You do not know Death – Life and Death. I do. Thus, your stage name was called.

The Spiritual Realm is warning you. Truly heed your warning or you will not like the consequences when Death come a knocking. And no, I am not threatening you. I am just delivering the Message therefore, your heart is truly not clean when it comes to the True and Living God.

<u>God is the giver of Life, but humans are the takers of life.</u>

<u>Humans take their own life thus, taking their life from God.</u>

Humans kill self not God kill humans. Thus, no human look at their sins; all the debt they've racked up here on Earth in the name of Death; their death.

God is real. It is us as humans that make God out to be unreal. It is us as humans that give dirty including, give dirty worship and praise.

Lady Saw stop mocking God. God is not a game. God is real.

Michelle

It's amazing how we as humans say God yet, deceive self in the interim.

It's amazing how many humans say God has saved them yet, deceive self and live as the deceived.

You know what let me stop here because my head is about to start, and I need to go back to sleep. I refuse to think of the Lies of Humans when it comes to God; the True and Living God literally.

Humans have absolutely no sense when it comes to Life and God.

Humans have absolutely no respect for God thus they use the name of God to gain what they want here on Earth through deceiving the masses with their lies, false teaching and preaching, story telling, and more.

Evil destroys, and evil will forever destroy humans because; humans are that gullible when it comes to God.

God is not a closed book yet, humans shut themselves off from God.

Why Lovey?
Why do humans shut themselves off from you?

Why do humans believe and not know?
Why do humans seek you in dirty places?

You are not dirty. So, why can't humans go into clean place and sit with you?

Why can't humans go into clean places and talk to you?

Are you that scarce that humans cannot find you?

Wow.

Soon, just You, Me, and Mother Earth will have breakfast in bed. So, let's hurry up and find a good and true place for us where I can design my own haven for us where we can have breakfast in our bed together.

Mother Earth I need my clean; truly clean, clear, and precious river and spring that is perfect and pure – void of all impurities.

Michelle

Aye Lovey I need a date.
Will you be my date for the day and night?
Will you dine with me?
Have breakfast, lunch, and dinner with me?

It's Valentine's Day Lovey.
Truly be my Valentine.

Hold me.
Touch me.
Comfort me.
Never leave me.

Dance with me.
Let's surround us with truth.
True harmony.

Grow with me true, and truthfully.
Rise with me true, and truthfully.
Be my true gain all around.

Take my hand.
Squeeze it.

Happy Valentine's Day my Love.
Happy Valentine's Day.

Michelle

Remember me as I remember you.
Teach me the goodness and truth of life.
Truly love me.
Never forsake me.

Take me as I am.
Imperfect am I on some days.
But does it really matter; my imperfections on some days?

Are you not my rose without the thorns?
Are you not my guide?
My truth?
Reason for living good and true?

Frail am I at times.
But you are my joy, true beauty.

Michelle
February 14, 2021

Sit with me by our river.
Clear and clean is the water.

Do you want to take a dip with me; swim?

Come in.
Let me bathe you.
Bless you,
Comfort you.

Water is of Life.
Let me give you life.
All the goodness from within.

Aye yes, the perfect white rose.
This I created.
It's from me to you.

Soft
Subtle
Sweet

The aroma tickles the senses.
Bring a smile to your face.

Create with me.
We are in the water.
Let life reign.
Truly rain.

Michelle
February 14, 2021

It's not 4am as yet and I cannot go back to sleep. Now, I am writing.

Good morning beautiful. How was your Valentine's Day yesterday?

Did you have a perfect day like I did?

Had breakfast, lunch, and dinner and I have to truly thank God, Mother Earth, my Children; all who made my day perfect.

Got candy, flowers, food, money, a teddy bear. Wow because no one could or did take my happiness away from me. I felt so special yesterday that I was happily saying I am special. Trust me, I am older, and it is now that I am enjoying my life in some way.

Listen, when you have God and your Children; Good Family around you, you are truly blessed. Therefore, cherish life and the moments you spend with your Good Family and True Friends. I've made God my true friend and trust me, yesterday was a perfect day for me.

Now enough about me.

Did you have breakfast, lunch, and dinner with anyone special?
Did you get flowers?
Candy?
All you wanted and needed on this day?

It's a new day for me and I am listening to <u>*GIVE IT ALL YOU GOT*</u> *by Beres Hammond.*

I will not keep this book too long. I truly do not need to.

<u>AUSTRALIA – CALIFORNIA DREAM</u>

I do not know what is going to happen with these lands. In the dream Australia, is going to burn – be destroyed in some way weather wise. I am not sure if drought is going to consume the land thus the burning of the land, but something bad is going to happen to Australia weather wise.

Know I did not see the devastation of Australia, but the land was destroyed somehow. So, for Australians, I would begin to ration water wise. Meaning, store up water from now so that when drought happen, you are prepared. More and more destruction is going to happen world wide because Mother Earth is not dicking around. She needs change; positive changes because Man – Humans have overdeveloped her without thinking of her life therefore, she too must ration.

She too (Mother Earth) must think of herself and her life. She cannot continue to allow humans to destroy her. She has a life too and humans refuse to think of her, and her life.

When it comes to humans everything is me, me, me; GREED. We treat Earth; Mother Earth like we own it – her, and not one human own Earth; Her.

As humans we buy land here on Earth but let me ask everyone in humanity this. What do you truly own here on Earth?

Did Mother Earth tell anyone of you you can buy her, or even own her?

So, what land do you own here on Earth?
Do you not die and leave all that you say you own behind?
What land can you take with you once your flesh is gone?
What land can you take with you once your spirit is gone?

So, what do you truly own here on Earth?
After you are gone, is Earth not still here?

So now tell me; can anyone outlive Life, and the Life of Earth?

<u>California, I did not see nor was California mentioned in the dream. It was Australia in the dream that was destroyed weather wise, but I am extending this dream to California weather wise. I do not know why, but I have to for some reason.</u>

Human life is not going to be the same because more death is truly coming. So, if you can help yourself today for tomorrow, then help yourself.

Know; tomorrow for me is not necessarily the next day, but a week, weeks, a month, months, a year, or years down the line. So, be prepared. I told you about the <u>GOD TRAIN in MINI BOOK.</u>

<u>Nations are locked out of the Kingdom of God thus, the tears many have to; must shed.</u>

Life is truly not a game thus billions truly do not think of their Spiritual Self.

I cannot worry about your Spiritual Self for you. You have to secure you. Yes, I have my Saved with God therefore, I need my seeds; the seeds God has and have given me to be safe and saved from all that is to come.

Yes, I need a true and clean environment for the saved therefore, Life must separate from Death here on Earth. The Saved of Life can no longer commune – live with those who are truly not saved by Me or God.

The Segregation and Separation of Life and Death must begin here on Earth therefore, we as the Good and True of Life must come together and secure each other so that when lands are being fully destroyed, we are truly safe and saved. Meaning, all that must and will happen to the unsaved, we are immune to it. We have food to eat, clean and pure water to drink. All that affects the Unsaved truly do not affect us.

We cannot say we are God's Children and People and continue to disobey God by not having a pure and clean environment for our self here on Earth.

We cannot say we are God's Children and People and continue to be integrated in the Systems of Death here on Earth. We have to; must separate and segregate our self from all facets of evil if we are to be saved.

We need our own land.
Our own good businesses.
Schools
Doctors
Farmers
People, and more.

The Good and True of Life – God's Children and People can no longer let the Wicked and Evil of Earth and the Spiritual Realm benefit off us.

Evil do consume life therefore, <u>AS CHILDREN AND PEOPLE OF GOD, WE ARE TO KNOW OUR PLACE WITH GOD, AND SEPARATE OUR SELF FROM THE EVIL ONES OF EARTH.</u>

<u>We have to have our own good and true domains here on Earth.</u>

We need to have our own __WAY OF LIVING.__

We need to __PUT GOD FIRST ABOVE ALL.__

We need to have our own:
Schools
Books
God
Hospitals for the time being.
Judicial System that is based on the Law and Laws of God not Man – Men.

We need to have our own:

Land and lands.
Grocery stores.
Restaurants and eateries.
Cars that are environmentally friendly.

Homes that are tax free. Meaning, we live free here on Earth without paying taxes.

Earth nor God tax us, therefore, we need to live free with God and Earth.

We need to build with God and Earth.
We need to think of God and Earth.
We need to have Good Children.
Good character, and content of character.
We need to have good and true people around us all the time.

We cannot put our self before God, Earth; the environment we are living in.

We need to have our own:

Good and true clothing designers.
Music
Talk

Walk
Stance
Truth, and more with God.

My body is feeling different therefore I am going to go back to bed. I so have to declutter my room. I have way too many things that have expired.

I so have to do things differently shopping wise. When I buy, I think of others and thinking of others is truly not helping of others because I buy, and these others cannot receive. I guess in this way, God and I are no different. I truly loathe having and not being able to give.

Usually, no forget it because I am forbidden to go to Jamaica thus, all I have for people is still here. I so have to find another route with God for giving.

I need true givers to give with me.

Givers that can travel with me to go to other lands and give. Lands God allow us to go into to give.

I truly love to give, and I refuse to go into anyone's land and give them Religion, or My God. I refuse to. My giving is truly not giving to get. My giving is true and will forever ever without end be true with God, and who get.

I truly miss giving. Yes, the environment of Earth has and have changed when it comes to humans, but I truly cannot think of this; the changing environment of humans.

It seems humans want to be controlled, and humans are being controlled.

I don't know but, <u>how can you live without seeing the environment around you?</u>

<u>How can you live with your eyes closed?</u>

Technology have and has massacred life thus, many truly cannot live by themselves, or live in silence. Many have to talk hence the different chatter in life for real.

Michelle
February 2021

I did go back to sleep and now it's the evening. I did some major cleaning of my room and it so look better. That clutter is not there on one side. Have to do the other side of my room.

I so truly need a library because I have so many books.

I am truly a book hoarder for real. Hopefully one day God will let us have a true library together.

Okay enough. I know you want to know if I had any dreams, and not to disappoint I did.

I truly do not know what is going on but something massive is going to happen death wise. No everyone; in all honesty, I truly do not know about these Diseased Scientists that develop viruses and diseases to kill <u>*YOU THE PEOPLE OF EARTH.*</u>

Therefore, due to these Diseased and Vile Beasts that plague human life scientifically, and more, there is massive death coming globally.

From the dream I know there is going to be a worldwide plague. However, I do not know if there is going to be worldwide earthquakes that sink lands with the people in it.

I know I saw a dead body in the ground, this Chinese Lady that looked as if she suffered from something that killed people. No, it's not like this scam – Covid-19 Scam. <u>*This PLAGUE AND OR, DISEASE IS TRULY GOING TO WIPE OUT PEOPLE HERE ON EARTH.*</u> *Like I said, I saw a dead body in the ground, this Chinese Lady that looked as if she suffered from something that killed people.*

I know there was massive death on land from this something; plague, virus, and or, disease. People were dying on a massive scale. Zombies do not describe these people in my view, but you would think so from what plagued them. And no, this is not a Zombie Dream or Movie.

People were trying to escape the land they lived in but were not permitted to leave. In the dream, all who tried to leave were eradicated; killed. Men; White Men would come after them and kill them.

In the dream, there was a cure for what afflicted the people. The cure was in England thus, people were trying to get to England for this cure. However, you could not fly, you were locked off from leaving. So instead, some took to the Sea to leave their land.

I will not analyze this dream because the dream is self explanatory. I did tell you in other books there is more diseases; viruses to come. Humans are wicked and Evil. Thus, Evil will never ever concede to Life – God. Evil will never stop being evil.

Evil have to have more time in the Domain of Death. So, all you see humans doing; is for Death, and a place in Hell with Death.

<u>Humans refuse to see the consequences of their sins because all think God – the God of Life is their bitch that would SACRIFICE A CHILD OF LIFE TO DEATH.</u>

And I will forever ever tell you. <u>GOD FOR WHOM I CALL LOVEY FROM TIME TO TIME IS NOT DEATH'S BITCH. NOR IS GOD THE BITCH OF HUMANS.</u>

GOD WOULD NEVER EVER SACRIFICE THE LIFE OF A CHILD OF LIFE TO SAVE YOU FROM YOUR SINS – DEATH.

LIFE HATH ABSOLUTELY NOTHING TO DO WITH DEATH IN THAT WAY. THUS, DEATH KEEP THE WICKED AND EVIL FROM GOD – LIFE.

No one evil can or will ever enter into the Kingdom and Domain of God – Lovey come on now.

You sin, why the hell should a Child of Life be sacrificed for your sinful and wicked ass?

Bleep you. You are not above God; nor are you above the Law and Laws of Life.

Every sin has and have a cost. Thus, the basic cost for one sin depending on the sin is:

24000 x 48000 years in Hell. The Hell you created for self here on Earth.

24 000 X 48 000 = 1, 152, 000 000.

Now tell me, why the hell should a Child of Life take on your burden – sins. It's only a fool that would go to hell for 1 billion one hundred and fifty two million years for just one of your sins. Plus, this basic value do not include the days, months, and years you've sinned for.

Hell no, keep your hell. Thus, God anno puppunennay for humans or anyone.

71

Keep your crosses and hell literally. God is not a fool. Thus, God protect every Child of Life. This I know for a fact without doubt.

God would never let a Child of Life save the wicked and evil, and <u>DEATH WOULD NEVER EVER LET GOD – ANYONE OF LIFE TAKE FROM DEATH. THUS, HUMANS TRULY DO NOT KNOW ABOUT BLACK FEMALE DEATH.</u>

Every Child of Life know or should know about Black Female Death. She's the one to warn you first if you are stopping her from doing her job. Meaning, you as a Chosen of Life here on Earth, if you stop Death from taking certain lands and people. She Black Female Death do not care. <u>SHE WILL KILL THE CHOSENS THAT INTERFERE IN DEATH. SHE WILL SINK THE LAND OF THE CHOSEN WITH THE PEOPLE THEM IN IT TOO.</u>

Thus, Female Black Death you truly do not interfere or mess with because she is that deadly. And yes, I did talk about Black Female Death in other books.

<u>Listen and know:</u>
God do not deal and will never deal in human and animal sacrifices.

God is not Babylonian therefore, <u>God KNOW NOT Abraham, and the Abrahamic Law and Laws of Human and Animal Sacrifices.</u>

God do not deal in Polygamy.
God do not deal in Incest.

Therefore, <u>NO BABYLONIAN</u> has ever entered the Realm, World, and Kingdoms of God. All of Babylon was/were and still are locked out of the Realm of God until this day.

So, know the truth of Satan's Creed; those lying Babylonians who say the are Jews but are of the <u>Syn</u>-agogues of Satan. Thus, to the Children and People of Life, <u>you know the truth, adhere to the Truth of God, and come out of the Realms of Babylon. You are being warned and told so truly listen.</u>

After that dream I did talk to Mother Earth my way. I told her she need to let go of Evil – all the evil in her that abuse, and do all to kill her.

Yes, I told her she have to respect herself. She have to and must think of her life. Humans care not for her therefore, she must have ambition for herself and walk away from humans.

Whether we as humans know it. Mother Earth is our Life Giver, Sustainer, and Maintainer here on Earth. Without Mother Earth we would not have water to drink, food to eat, herbs to heal us, and more.

Mother Earth give us all that is of life physically and it is us as humans that destroy all the goodness she has been giving us here on Earth; well, in her.

Thus, in this sense. THE SPIRITUAL IS SEPARATED FROM THE PHYSICAL.

Some of you will not comprehend my statement but, if you are not of Life you will not comprehend the separation of the Spiritual and Physical in this sense.

Sins are dirty thus, it's our sins that keep us from God here on Earth. Humans know not time thus, because we know not time, we cannot find God in that way. Thus, the Time here on Earth is different from Spiritual Time – the Time of God.

So yes, THE WICKEDNESS OF THE WHITE RACE – WHITE PEOPLE IS NOT YET DONE.

THEY HAVE TO CONTINUE TO KILL UNTIL THEIR END – they fulfill their book - bible.

So yes, Mother Earth have to think of herself because no humans is truly thinking about her and her life.

Not one here on Earth has ever said to Mother Earth, Mama, or Mother Earth; what can I do for you today to help you, clean you, sustain and maintain your life, and more?

Not one human think of Mother Earth as the keeper and sustainer of their life.

None here on Earth think to save Mother Earth from the Sins and atrocities each one of us do in her.

Instead of saving Mother Earth, humans do all to kill her. Therefore, Mother Earth have to abandon humans. She must now think of her life and save herself from humans.

Humans care not for her therefore, humans deplete all in her.

Humans take and take and cannot replace, and will never ever replace good and true when it comes to her.

Humans are truly wicked and evil unto her; Mother Earth thus, humans neglect her needs, cannot see her, cannot help her, cannot do good for her, or unto her.

So no, if Nations care not for her, then she must give up all that kill her; cause her true pain.

No, look at the way we as humans plant.

Look how humans develop diseases, viruses, plagues, chemicals, nuclear weapons, weapons, hate, live in hate, and more.

Humans are truly not good for life or to life.

Humans are Death – the TRUE KILLERS OF LIFE.

And none of you dare say; well God created Death.

God did not create death because; GOD DID NOT LAY WITH ANY OF YOU TO PROCREATE WITH THE LOTS OF YOU TO HAVE WICKED AND EVIL CHILDREN.

You found someone; shagged with each other to procreate – bring forth your child; children. Now let me ask you this; when you were shagging him *or her, where was God in the midst of your shagging?*

And don't you dare looked wide eyed at me. By now you should know that absolutely nothing is off limits to me and God, and the way I write. *And no, no one can lay with God. It is a Sin.* Thus, your Jesus bullshit story truly do not wash when it comes to God fathering a Child with Mary.

Thus, *humans do not know how energy work in the Black Female.*

Not one human can say; *GOD FATHERED, OR MOTHERED THEIR CHILD.*

God do not give evil. Humans give all that is wicked and evil.

You know what let me stop because; my concern right now is Mother Earth, the Saved of Life, Lovey, Me, and more.

So yes, if you as humans think this is it, had truly better think again literally.

Armageddon must come for the White Race Globally, and it is you the Citizens of each Land here on Earth that must pay, and pay dearly with your life.

Michelle
February 2021

Listen Black People it's time to stop thinking foolishly. Now I am losing my train of thought.

As Blacks – those who are true to life and of life. You cannot accept or believe in the Jesus Story anymore because God did not father a child with Mary, nor is Jesus God.

If you believe God <u>FATHERED A CHILD WITH MARY, THEN YOU WOULD HAVE COMMITTED SIN. A GRAVE SIN AGAINST GOD.</u>

If you believe God <u>FATHERED A CHILD WITH MARY, THEN YOU WOULD HAVE ACCEPTED THE LIES OF THE WHITE RACE THUS, COMMITTING SIN; A GRAVE SIN AGAINST GOD.</u>

Listen, we've all been given the lying story of Jesus to believe in thus, I need Africans to tell the true truth about Life and God if they know how to.

Africans so dyam lie, you truly have to wonder about them for real.

Listen, no one can keep the Lies of Africa and the White Race and think God is going to save them. Thus know; <u>GOD CANNOT PROCREATE WITH HUMANS. NOR WOULD GOD PROCREATE WITH HUMANS IN THAT WAY OR ANYWAY.</u>

<u>Humans are not clean.</u> *Therefore, God cannot procreate, or create with unclean beings; humans. God is clean and to put*

God on our dirty level it is a true sin. Therefore, go to God for forgiveness of this sin. Believing God procreated with a human and brought forth a child. Thus, know what the Holy Ghost as taught by man is. Spirits cannot procreate with humans in that way.

Energy is important to life *therefore, the Black Female is truly different from other nations. I've told you in other books that the* "*BLACK FEMALE CAN PRODUCE A CHILD WITHOUT THE UNION OF SPERM – THE SPERM AND EGG.*" *Thus, know the Story of Mary. The White Race cannot tell you the Black Female about you because they truly do not know your genetic makeup thus their DNA BULLSHIT.*

If humans – man could map the Human Genome as they call it then; *HUMANS WOULD FIND THE SPIRIT AND COULD MAP THE SPIRIT OF MAN – EVERY HUMAN ON THE FACE OF THIS PLANET.*

Therefore, as Black People; we need to know what we are doing, and presently none in the Black Race know what they are doing.

Now listen to me and it matters not if you truly do not like me. Know the truth of life.

Now, all you see happening here with….no, let me not say that. Let me say this.

AS BLACK PEOPLE, WE HAVE TO SHAPE AND TRAIN OUR THINKING DIFFERENTLY THUS; WE NEED TO FIND KNOWLEDGE – THE TRUTH OF THE BLACK RACE FROM THE

BEGINNING AND MOVING FORWARD IN LIFE.

Okay now listen.

Slavery
Racism
Prejudice
Religion
Religious Lies
Religious Division
Religious Inclusion
The Lies told on God
Politics
Conflict
War
Educational Lies
Mathematical Lies
Earthly Lies
Spiritual Lies
Economic Division
Mental Division
Sociological Division
Psychological Division
Psychological Brainwashing
Conditioning
Mental Genocide
Pharmaceutical and Corporate Lies
Genetic Lies
Generational Lies, and a lot more.

All was meant to keep you in the Black Race because, I am talking to you in the Black Race now; from the truth. All was given to you to keep you thinking, and believing in lies thus; KEEPING YOU AWAY FROM THE TRUTH AND THE TRUTH OF GOD – LIFE.

Once you keep believing in lies especially RELIGIOUS LIES, *you cannot and will never attain life. You must die – are going to die thus I told you, billions are going to die and it's over 100 million that will be saved. This is how I saw it and know it, and this is how I am relating it back to you.*

THE JOB OF EVIL IS EVIL.
EVIL MUST KEEP YOU FROM GOD.

EVIL MUST KEEP YOU FROM ATTAINING LIFE.

And say it by saying; "well what are you doing," and let me blast you?

Think and know the truth. Africa is truly not telling the truth because whether you like it or not, MANY IN AFRICA DID GIVE UP THEIR LIFE AND THIS THEY REFUSE TO TELL YOU – LET YOU KNOW.

IF YOU DO NOT KNOW THE TRUTH OF LIFE YOU CANNOT ATTAIN LIFE – GOD, *and this you truly need to know.*

The White Race has and have done their job. Billions in the Black Race did forfeit their life thus I tell you, I refuse to save any Sell Out Blacks.

We cannot say we are of God – Life and live like the dead.

Blacks continually accept the lies of Death – Evil and think these lies are going to save you/them. These lies are not saving you they are killing you. Therefore, it is truly wrong to be or want to be included in societies that are based on lies, as well as, give lies for you to live in, live by, die in, and die by.

Yes, lies are what we are given to live by, but it does not mean you of yourself cannot go to God for forgiveness as well as, the truth.

Evil fear God because God show you and tell you the truth. Once you know the Truth of Life, you won't need evil because now you have life – can live. Plus, you can no longer be deceived. Therefore, you were told not to question God. But, I am telling you categorically to:

QUESTION GOD.
GO TO GOD FOR THE TRUTH.

GO TO GOD FOR ALL YOUR NEEDS AND WANTS.

Man – humans lie, but God cannot lie to you because:

"TRUTH IS EVERLASTING LIFE."

Hey, you did not think you can sin against God did you?

Well, we do sin against God. When we/you accept religion, and the lies of religion; then you are sinning against God. You believe that God is as nasty, and stupid as Man depicted God in their so-called holy bible. Therefore, none that is associated with religion can enter, or will enter the Kingdom and Domain of God. This you all can take to the bank without doubt. This is how I saw it, and this is how I am relating it back to you.

God is with none in Religion. So, if you think you are saved, *TRULY CHECK YOUR SIN – DEATH RECORD WITH DEATH.*

If God have/has not forgiven you of your Sins done unto God; how will you be saved?

God cannot save you if you are not forgiven of your GOD SINS.

Therefore, *CHECK YOUR GOD SINS WITH GOD IF YOU CAN.*

Further, and now. Because Blacks have and has failed God, Successorship of Life fall on the Chinese – Mongolian Nation. So now, because; <u>Blacks have and has failed God, the Devil truly do not have to worry about Black People anymore.</u> Evil – the Devil did their Job, and took Blacks from God, <u>now the focus is on the Chinese and or, Mongolian Race.</u>

The White Race – all who fall under the White Banner of Death must cause China and or, the Mongolian and or, Chinese Race to fail – fall.

The White Race must do all for the Mongolian and or, Chinese Race to fail Life just like they caused Blacks to fail Life.

This is the Final Task for and of Evil; to make the next Successor and or, Nation that Life go to fail. I know this, it is you in the Global Community that do not know this.

Evil will never accept Life – God. Therefore, many here on Earth live to kill. Some are paid to kill. See your gangs, hired assassins, different armies, and religious armies of death, some of you who are mass murderers, liars, and more.

Therefore, Evil will always take from Life – You.

Evil live by lies therefore, those who are of Death must lie to you to get you to give up your spiritual, and physical life here on Earth.

Like I've told you, your sins come with a cost. It is you the human that truly do not know the cost of each sin. And, I did give you the cost of each sin in THE NEW BOOK OF KNOWLEDGE BOOK ONE AND TWO.

Life is our gain.
Death is our death.

So yes, as Black People we've forgotten the importance of OUR ENERGY, OUR VIBE, OUR LIFE, AND OUR GOD on a whole.

83

Like I said in other books, I did complete the task – that which God required of me thus; **THE NEW BOOK OF KNOWLEDGE BOOKS ONE AND TWO.**

As for the Sell Out Blacks of the Globe, I saved not one of you because. My job was not to save you nor did I want, or need to save any of you. **We are Blacks not White.** *Therefore, the White Man's God and Life is truly not ours.*

Whoredom is not a part of Life – the Life of God.
Sin is not a part of Life – the Life of God.
Death is not a part of Life – the Life of God.

The White Race is LOCKED OUT OF LIFE. Therefore, Life is not Life for everyone. Not everyone hath life and you need to know this.

Therefore, Life is life, and Death is death.

God cannot save those who are not of Life because some are of Death; live and do the bidding of Death.

You know, in all we as humans do. Billions live for Death without knowing it. I am sure if billions could see hell, their hell; they would be singing a different tune literally.

Our thoughts are real and they; our thoughts do influence not just our Physical Life here on Earth but they; our thoughts do affect our Spiritual Life.

Yes, it's sad that the Physical and Spiritual is separated. Many of you will not comprehend this because many do not know how Energy work, and who God truly is.

So yes, both worlds are separated; the Physical and Spiritual World in the truest of sense but when it comes to humans – those who were procreated both worlds are not separated thus, the physical and spiritual conflicts we have with self, and each other here on Earth.

Michelle
February 2021

Listen Black People; while you were there fighting to be included in societies of injustice, the Devil was busy gaining success off you. Not one of you know that absolutely no one that is of Life – the Life of God can fight to be included in the Devil's Domain.

Life is not Death.

Death is Death therefore, many in the Black Race have and has been played, and they don't even know it.

While you were being busy fighting to be included in unjust societies globally, the Devil and their people were busy creating descension in your hearts, land, communities you live in, in your home, in your children, the education systems of lies they gave you, and more.

While you were busy fighting and killing each other, Death was more than happy, and more than busy adding your name to the Book of Death. Plus, more than busy calculating the amount of time you must spend in your hell burning for disobedience – all the sins you've done here on Earth.

While you were busy trying to be included in the Devil's Systems Globally, the Devil was smiling all the way to the bank because the Devil made sure you were excluded out of life – the Life of God.

While you were busy building the Devil, the Devil was doing all to deceive you by ensuring God moves further away from you.

While you were busy fighting the system and saying the system is unfair and unjust, the Devil and their people were keeping you from God.

While you were busy fighting and running behind your political and religious leaders, they; the Devil was busy ensuring that you have no life here on Earth, and in the Spiritual Realm with God.

While you were crying about how unfair your political leaders are, you were not looking at yourself. You still cannot see that Evil CANNOT ENSURE YOUR SAFETY IN LIFE.

While you in the Black Race were busy absorbing their God – Spell; Gospel, the Devil and their people were busy securing your place with them in hell.

While you were busy all around, none of you could see the Devil decimating you, your land, your health, your future not with self and others, but with God.

Thus, you still cannot see the Devil and their People were busy decimating you and your land.

You still cannot see that your Economic Growth, and Spiritual Growth land wise, economic wise, food wise, water wise, weather wise, environmental wise, and more were being taken from you.

<u>Listen and know:</u>

EVIL WILL NEVER ENSURE YOU ARE FED PROPERLY.

EVIL WILL NEVER ENSURE YOU HAVE ENOUGH FOOD TO EAT.

EVIL WILL NEVER ENSURE YOU HAVE PROPER HOUSING.

<u>Thus, EVIL ENSURES THE LIES THEY FEED YOU, YOU ACCEPT; CRAVE, LIVE BY, AND DIE BY.</u>

None can see Evil because, to many; Humans are humans, and God forgive all without knowing God cannot forgive evil – the evils of man and spirit.

While you were busy being busy, the Devil was doing all to take you from Life. As humans we are the ones to incorporate evil in our life.

We are the ones to allow evil to take us from life so, you cannot blame evil for all the evils done unto you. You have to blame self – you.

Technology – Man's Technology is truly not our gain. Figure it out.

Now, look who oversee you religiously, and politically.

Look who oversee your household because many if not all of you say, "the MAN IS THE HEAD OF THE HOUSEHOLD."

Once you know the truth, you are a threat to those who run the World. Thus, you are now on their eliminated list. You must be eliminated at all cost because the Children and People of Death have to; must have you believing in their lies. It's their form of Control – Dominion over you.

Once you know the truth and begin to live by the truth, your goodness grow thus, you are taking you from Death. And yes, not all can take self from Death because of the Contract they signed with Death.

Listen, it is us as humans that put others above us.
We as humans that allow ourselves to be dominated and control.

God cannot put a man or woman to oversee you, nor do God dominate and control you, so why are we as humans allowing unclean beasts; humans to dominate and control us?

Why do we as humans put unclean beasts; humans above us?

Domination and Control is truly not in the vocabulary of God so, why are we allowing men to control and dominate us when men are truly not clean. Yes, I know not all, but seek not control or domination. Meaning, seek not to be controlled and dominated. There is absolutely no freedom in Domination; Dominion and Control. Nor, did God tell anyone to control and dominate anyone; each other.

As humans we need freedom, and if you have not freedom then, you are a slave to the system; the different systems set up by men and yes, some women to dominate and control you.

It's February 22, 2021 and it's snowing outside. It doesn't bother me because right now where I am at, it is blessed I would say, and I truly thank God for this. I have food to eat, water to drink, my children with me, not all but my children are with me so, I have absolutely nothing to worry about right now. Yes, I have my bills, but I am truly not worried about them.

I am free therefore, I truly do not let this pandemic bother me, and will never let it bother me. I know how to live by myself, and with me therefore, I am truly good to go. God has and have truly provided for me therefore God is my rely on, and go to.

MY DREAM WAKING DREAM

This morning though. I am not sure if I was dream waking. You will not understand dream waking. I am not sure if I was seeing this via my dream world or via my waking state visons.

I am not sure if I was dream waking when I saw to the South of Me this huge and or, massive ball of fire. Think explosion – something exploded. So, from here to Niagara Falls to Buffalo, New York, I am not sure if a plant is going to explode and or, what is going to happen somewhere in the United States of America to see something explode. Nor am I sure if there is going to be massive drought or fires in the United States and Canada.

I will not put anything to it because sleep wake accounts I cannot pinpoint, nor do I put much emphasis or merit on them.

Listen, I write and send out books to people in hope that who I send these books to will do something to inform all who I speak about including, warn you the people. I do not have Facebook, and will never ever in this lifetime or another lifetime have Facebook.

I more than categorically refuse this platform more than infinitely and indefinitely more than forever ever without end.

If Facebook was the last platform on the face of this planet, I still would not have it. God how I more than loathe this platform to no end. This is me. You are different. Just because I more than loathe a platform, you do not have to. Do you, that which pleases you. For me, I see no benefit in Facebook. Yes, I did have Facebook once upon a time when it first came out but due to nastiness – the unclean, and nasty postings some people posted, I quickly gave it up. Certain things I refuse in my life thus, many young Black Females have nor morals. or moral value to what they will do to get notices and likes.

I do have a Twitter account for which I have not used in years.

Deleted my LinkedIn account with LinkedIn years ago.

I do not have Instagram, nor do I have a Web Page. Tried years ago to make one; a Web Page with Wix, and did, but failed miserably.

I am what you call a dinosaur when it comes to technology. I truly loathe Technology. All that is negative I find in the Technology of Man. For me and to me, Technology has and have taken away from the family.

Technology is Death because, man use their so-called Technology in their killing spree.

Technology is intrusive and invasive therefore humans have no control over their life; lives. Technology is the Death of Humans – the Human Death Trap, and I am so going to leave it at this. Technology, I can do and truly live without thus, I am truly limited Technology Wise.

Don't need it therefore I do my best to do without it. So, if you are seeking to find me on the different platforms of your life technology wise, you will not find me I hope. And if you are thinking it. I am one of the select few that truly do not have a cellphone. Don't want one or need one but unfortunately, I am going to have to eventually get one, but if I can help it, I am hoping to be in the area where God truly need me to be so that I truly do not have to get one; a cellphone.

Man do I need to live off the grid of man. I need to be on the Grid of God and yes, Mother Earth living a good and true life. So yes, Technology I can truly do without. You can't but I truly can. I truly don't need to be in the know. I see and know via my dream world, and the different outlets of life already.

Michelle
February 2021

BOOKS BY MICHELLE JEAN 2021

MY TALK JANUARY 2021

MY TALK JANUARY 2021 – BOOK TWO

MINI BOOK

COMING SOON

A LITTLE TALK WITH MOTHER EARTH